THE WADSLEY THAT WAS

First published in 1999 by
Monteney Community Workshop
Sheffield

ISBN 1 872934 56 0

Monteney Community Workshop
49, Morral Road
Sheffield, S5 9AJ.

“Drawn From Memory”

So if you find what’s called a blunder
Let what you see cause you to wonder!
Is old Wadsley far too late?
Or does my pencil cause debate?

The Wadsley That Was

My pen strolls down memory lane
For dear old Wadsley is not the same
They say that we must move ahead
Whilst yesteryear is killed stone dead.

The cottages at the top of Coal Pit Lane, approximately 1935

Luke Lane from Bower's Corner with Coal Pit Lane and Bland Lane in the Background
Approximately 1945

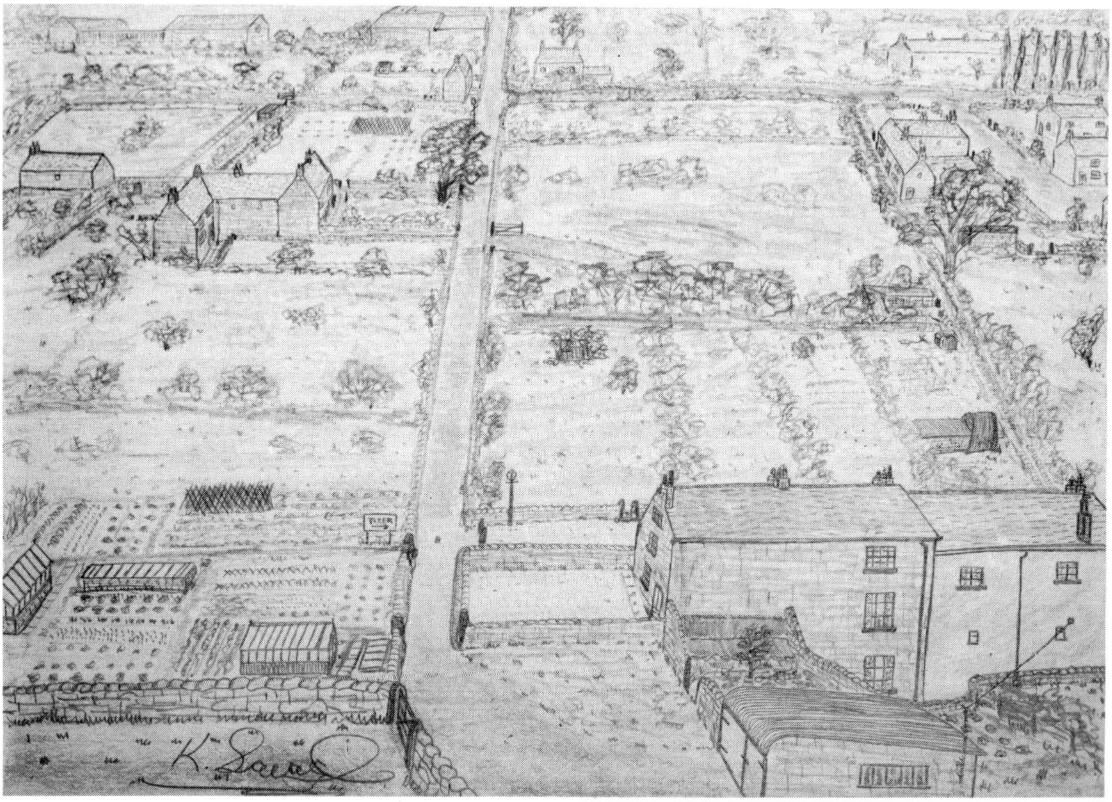

Looking Down Coal Pit Lane, approximately 1949

Bottom Farm, at junction of Luke Lane and Water Lane, approximately 1945

Coal Pit Lane, Luke Lane,
Water Lane and Bland Lane
Many more besides.
Brushed aside in madness
Before our very eyes.

The Baker's shop, the Cobbler's place
And the well known General Store
Yes! In spite of protest
Now lost to modern bore.

The local shop, more commonly known as "Nelly Betn'ys", approximately 1959

An inside view of the village shop, approximately 1959

So pray my “God” my pencil reminisce
Those bygone values must persist
For if our heritage is to remain
And things that matter stay the same
Then we must stop, think and wonder
Why keep repeating the big blunder?

A village of folk that knew one another,
Best have no shame or tell your mother.
Gossip, they dare not make
In case it were dealt onto their own plate.

Wadsley Parish Church the School and the Mission Room, approximately 1920

The village school and Wadsley Church
Where there was joy and where there was hurt.
School yard games and congregations,
A meeting point for conversations.

Old Wadsley Common with its Robin Hood's Den,
Childhood games of his merry men.
Bilberries galore and things to explore.
Could any child wish for anything more?

Once a year the Wadsley Fete
Burst a balloon or smash a plate.
Oh! What excitement and old fashioned fun.
On Studfield Hill we all would run.

A village of charm is what I recall
With stone built cottages
And the Squire's Hall.
Why can't we ever seem to learn?
For when our heritage we do burn
The good old days can never return.

Normandale House, the Blue Bell Wood and Top Farm at the end of Quaker Lane, approximately 1929

Looking up at the yard at the top of Coal Pit Lane, approximately 1959

In spite of all we should rejoice
At least while pencils draw their voice.
Drawing a record of what's gone by
A quiet expression of why we cry.
An ordinary village of childhood days,
A precious chance to mend our ways.

Oh, dear old Wadsley village
Thy streets and charm we all do pillage
But in my memory you are quite safe.
Yes, Wadsley was a special place
And if my memory does me fail
Then pray my pencil tells the tale.

The Star Inn and barber's shop, approximately 1959

The corner of Luke Lane, locally known as Bower's Corner, approximately 1958

Looking up at Coal Pit Lane, leading to Wadsley Common, approximately 1945

The local "Ganister Quarry" on Studfield Hill, approximately 1945

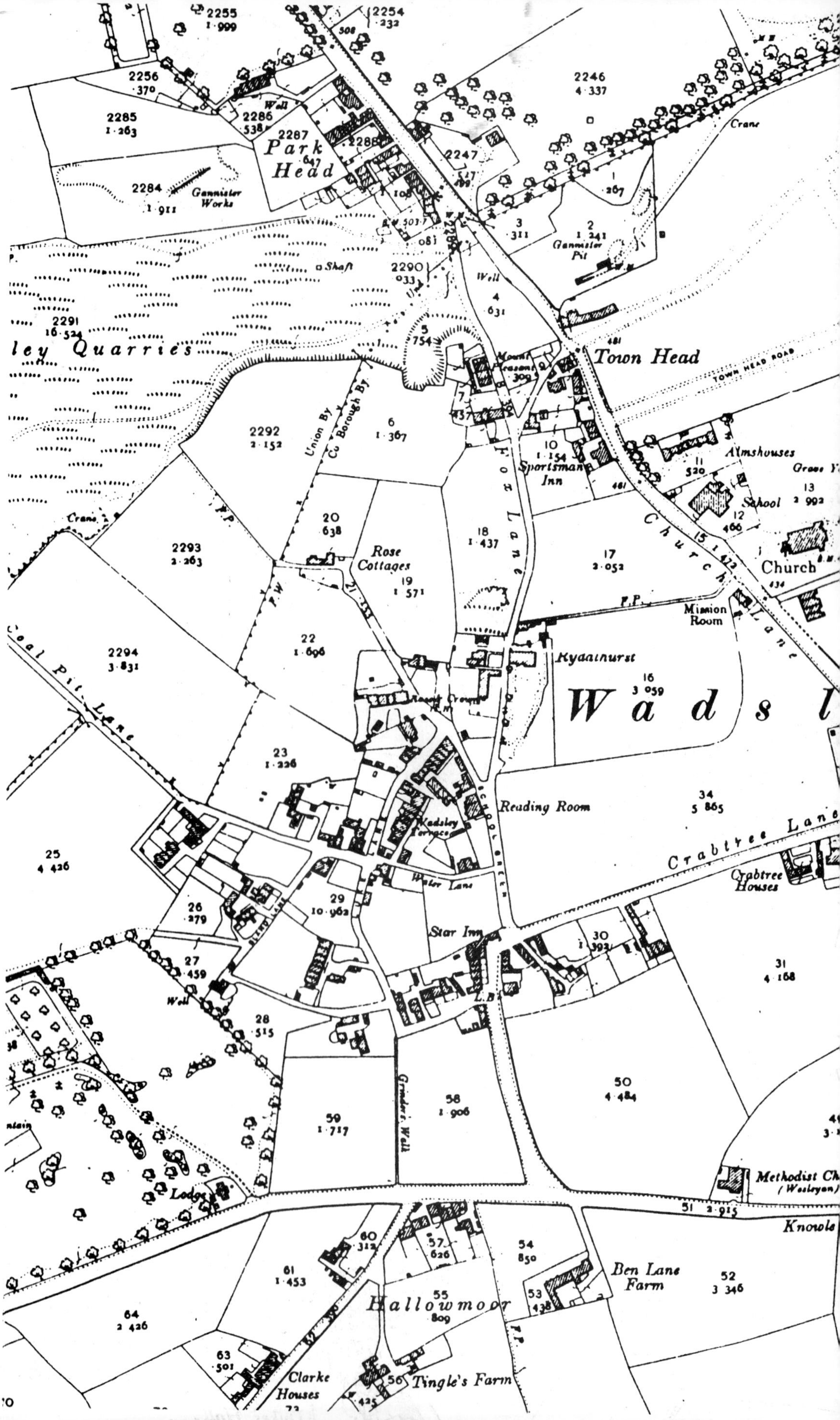

Park Head
Gannister Works
Shaft
Well
Gannister Pit
Crane
ley Quarries
Town Head
Town Head Road
Mount Pleasant
Union By
Co Borough By
Fox Lane
Sportsman Inn
Almshouses
School
Church
Church Lane
Rose Cottages
Mission Room
Rydalhurst
Wadsl
Coal Pit Lane
Rose & Crown
Reading Room
Crabtree Lane
Crabtree Houses
Wadsley Terrace
Water Lane
Star Inn
L.B.
Well
Grinder's Well
Lodge
Methodist Ch (Wesleyan)
Knowle
Ben Lane Farm
Hallowmoor
Clarke Houses
Tingle's Farm

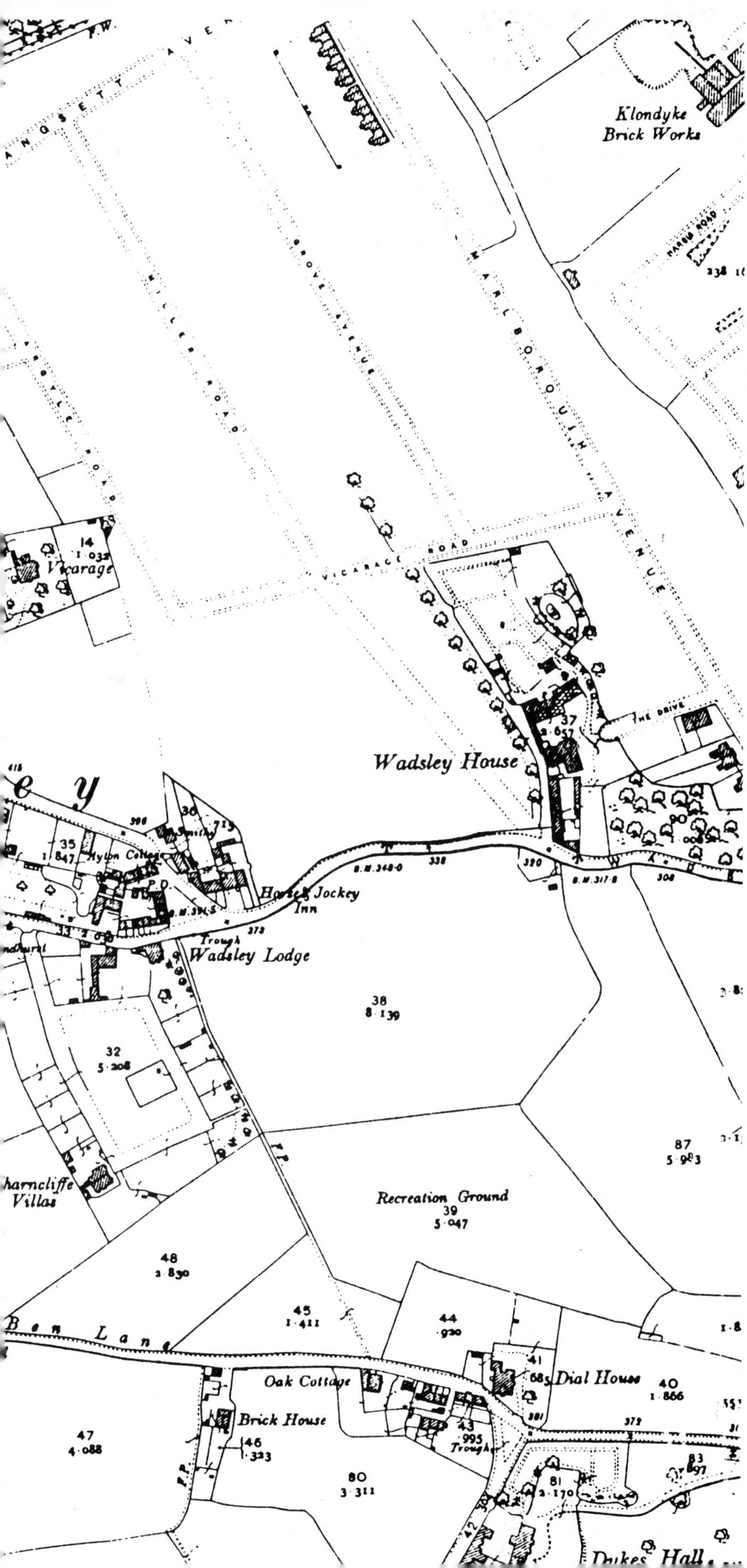

Map of Wadsley, as it was, around the end of the nineteenth century.

Now Millennium bugs and high-tech. lives
May surely cause real pain
So just let go of computer jives
Turn Wadsley's loss into gain.

Now don’t despair, just be aware
That our heritage we must care.
We need not again our future wrong
But rather stay as we belong.

The Cobbler's Place, looking up Water Lane from Rural Lane

The local bread shop on Luke Lane, approximately 1929

So when we sit upon reflection
Let's be sure to make correction.
Is it high-tech. or Millennium mayhem?
Or is it the fact we continue to make'em?

Cottages on Water Lane, known locally as "The Ratton Row", approximately 1953

Stour Lane from Rural Lane, approximately 1945

Wadsley Village, from Rural Lane, approximately 1945

The village shop on Luke Lane, and the local pub, known as the Top House, approximately 1947

‘Tis a mixture of sadness and joy
To have known dear old Wadsley when I was a boy
And as my memory with thanks does surrender
All Wadsleys that was, we must remember.....

Out of Wadsley

Out of Wadsley came many a lad
None of whom were one bit glad
Alas all were mighty sad
When from old Wadsley they were torn
The place now gone where they were born.

The inside of our house, approximately 1951

Out of Wadsley came many a lass
None of whom you could surpass
When they reflected on the past.
Yes! With their men folk they too went.
Men make decisions, women must relent.

A typical kitchen, approximately 1951

Out of Wadsley came many a yarn
Some of which were not so calm.
Once there was a Wadsley ghost
So the locals did so boast
Until their stories then turned foul
When they discovered a huge white owl!

Out of Wadsley came many a load
Of quarry stone for one's abode.
In the quarry men would toil
And in the end their health would spoil.
Many claimed it to be the dust
But a few with wealth said it was a must,
For the stone was needed for many a call
To help build Wadsley with its Squire Hall.

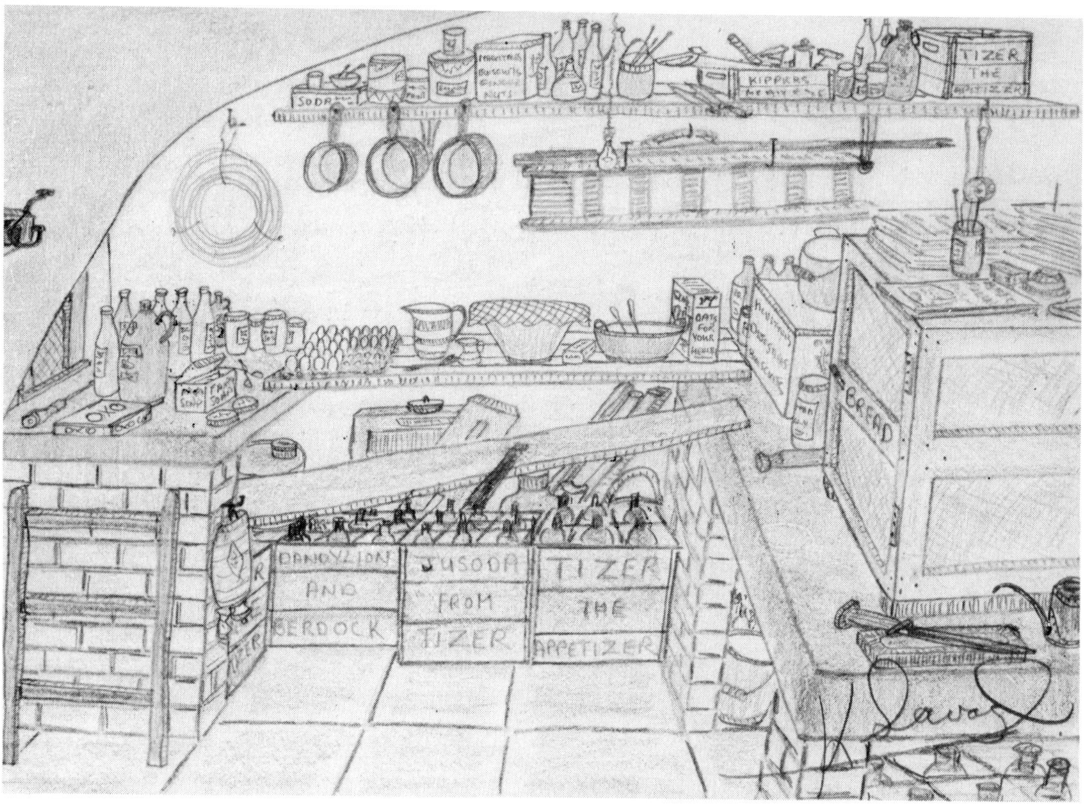

The pantry, inside our house approximately 1951

Out of Wadsley some knew war.
Many a campaign including the 'Bore'
Some returned and brought much pride
Whilst others on the battle field died.
Yes! Old Wadsley has also cried
A simple truth that should never be denied.

Out of Wadsley came many joys
Especially at Christmas with home made toys.
Wadsley carols and New Year rhymes.
Yes, there were many happy times.
Bonfire night and fireworks bright,
Much excitement. What a delight!
Neighbours rallied and joined in the fun
And Wadsley smiled on everyone.

Inside our house; looking up the yard from inside the porch
approximately 1951

Out of Wadsley the spirit now gone,
Lives contented and faces that shone.
Shunned to make room for house improvement.
Now like clocks without a movement
Do I hear you say let go?
That yesteryear was too slow?
If I do then have a mind.
The pace of life might seem a bind,
But only if we check our pace
Will all our 'Wadsleys' remain safe.

Wadsley Co-op and a cutler's workshop, the bottom of Stour Lane, approximately 1951

WE ARE SURVIVORS
(FOR THOSE BORN BEFORE 1945)

We were born before television, before penicillin, polio shots, frozen foods, Xerox, plastic, contact lenses, videos, frisbees and the Pill. We were before the radar, credit cards, split atoms, lazer beams and ball point pens; before dishwashers, tumble dryers, electric blankets, air conditioners, drip dry clothes......and before man walked on the moon.
We got married first and then lived together (how quaint can you be?). We thought 'fast food' was what you ate in Lent, a 'Big Mac' was an oversized raincoat and 'crumpet' we had for tea. We existed before house husbands, computer dating, dual cars and when a 'meaningful relationship' meant getting along with cousins and 'sheltered accommodation' was where you waited for a bus.

We were before the day care centres, group homes and disposable nappies. We never heard of FM radio, tape decks, electric typewriters, artificial hearts, word processors, yogurt, or young men wearing earrings. For us 'time sharing' meant togetherness, a 'chip' was a piece of wood or fried potato, 'hardware' was nuts and bolts and software wasn't a word.

Before 1945 'Made in Japan' meant junk, the term 'making out' referred to how you did in your exams, 'stud' was something that fastened a collar to a shirt and 'going all the way' meant staying on a double-decker to the bus depot. Pizzas, McDonalds and instant coffee were unheard of. In our day cigarette smoking was fashionable, 'grass' was mown, 'coke' was kept in a coal house, a 'joint' was a piece of meat you ate on Sundays and 'pot' was something you cooked in. 'Rock music' was a fond mother's lullaby, 'Elderado' was an ice cream, a 'gay person' was the life and soul of the party and nothing more, while 'aids' just meant beauty treatment or help for someone in trouble.

We who were born before 1945 must be a hardy bunch when you think of the way in which the world has changed and the adjustments we have had to make. No wonder we are so confused and there is a generation gap today.....BUT

By the grace of God.......we have survived! **Hallelujah**